EFFECTIVE DELEGATION

Save time and boost quality at work

Written by Véronique Bronckart
Translated by Rebecca Neal

Coaching 50MINUTES.com

DELEGATE SUCCESSFULLY

- **Issue:** how can I effectively entrust my colleagues with tasks and responsibilities?
- **Uses:** delegating tasks to your colleagues allows you to save time on a project, but also to motivate them and cultivate their talents in order to give the project the best possible chance of success.
- **Professional context:** project management, team management, etc.
- **FAQs:**
  - I don't feel like I have too much work, do I still need to delegate?
  - When is the right time to delegate?
  - When I delegate, am I abandoning part of the project?
  - Can I entrust my colleagues with any kind of tasks?
  - Once a task has been delegated, do I still need to deal with it?
  - What tools can help me to organise my delegating?
  - What risks are linked to delegating?
  - How can I make sure my coworker will accept this task positively?
  - Can delegation be revoked partway through a project?
  - Do I need to formalise my delegation in writing?

For many people, delegating means "losing control". Out of fear of disturbing other people or a lack of confidence, or simply to ensure that a project is carried out in line with their own expectations and conditions, they try to undertake the assignment alone. However, in this situation the danger of being overwhelmed by the number of tasks to complete and of not accomplishing the goal set, or even of experiencing burnout, is never far away.

To avoid this kind of situation, a good project manager will have mastered the art of delegating effectively. Indeed, their role is not to keep a stranglehold on each component part of the project, but to oversee the project as a whole. Entrusting as many tasks as possible to other people will allow them to avoid overload and stress, which could hinder the accomplishment of the project, and to focus on the most important activities. Furthermore, delegating lets them demonstrate trust in the members of their team. The team members will feel involved, which will motivate and empower them. Everyone wins!

However, the decision to delegate should not be taken lightly or hastily, as this risks harming the project and dissuading you from delegating again. Do not be afraid to rely on your colleagues and learn the rules to follow and the behaviour to adopt towards your teammates in order to delegate without fear and successfully carry out your project.

EFFECTIVE DELEGATION: THE BASICS

WHAT IS DELEGATION?

Handing over responsibility

The first thing to avoid is confusing delegation with the division of tasks, because these two processes are very different. Delegating involves entrusting one or two tasks (or objectives, because actions follow on from objectives) to one or more colleagues by making them aware of their responsibilities. It does not mean abandoning a project, losing control of it, decentralising it or losing power, but rather sharing the carrying out of the project in order to achieve a better final result.

The concept of responsibility is essential here. When you assign a task to a colleague, they must be able to enjoy some freedom to make decisions. They must be able to proceed as they want in order to reach the goal set. If they do not have this decision-making power, you will not be delegating but simply giving an order to a subordinate. However, although your colleague is responsible for accomplishing their objective, you are still responsible for the activities and decisions of the person you have delegated the task to. This is why you should have complete trust in the person you have selected and ensure some degree of monitoring to make sure that the objectives are reached.

- Temporary delegation is the most common form of delegation. Indeed, subordinates frequently replace the superior responsible for decisions when the latter is absent, or when their services are requested because their skills are needed. In this case, the concepts of decision-making and authority are separated: the subordinate makes decisions during the delegation period, but they are not responsible for the consequences.
- Permanent delegation involves granting long-term decision-making power in certain situations which are defined beforehand. The concepts of decision-making and responsibility are linked: the colleague must therefore take responsibility for the consequences of their actions. In this case, providing for an additional clause in the colleague's contract is advised.

Management styles

Delegation is influenced and facilitated by the kind of management used within the company. Management can be:

- **Directive.** This management style is very structured, and involves precise instructions and orders. The employee generally does not have any real decision-making power, which is not very motivating. This is not strictly speaking delegation, but rather the transmission of orders concerning a task to be carried out.

- **Explanatory.** This aims to mobilise employees. Orders and instructions are precise and accompanied by explanations and justifications of the decisions made. Colleagues have a low level of autonomy, which can slow down the process of project development.
- **Participative.** This style is based on relationships. Although it may seem somewhat disordered, it proves relatively efficient. Decisions are made in consultation with colleagues, which motivates them and encourages them to become invested in the project.
- **'Delegative'.** This kind of management, based on the manager's trust in their team, relies on responsibility, independence, initiative and decision-making. Team members then feel valued and invested in the project.

Each management style has its strengths and weaknesses. The whole art of good team leadership is being able to switch from one style to another depending on the person you are dealing with and the situation. Obviously, the 'delegative' style is best for encouraging delegation between a supervisor and their team.

The law of division of labour

Many managers have lost faith in delegation and will find a thousand excuses to avoid it: "It's too much responsibility for employees", "The task won't get done correctly", "Explaining everything would take too long". In doing this, they quickly forget a small but vitally important detail: delegating responds to the law of division of labour. The division of labour, which was theorised by Adam Smith (British Enlightenment economist, 1723-1790), involves dividing up a single complex task into several tasks which will then be carried out by different specialists. Logically, a person focusing on a specific task will be more efficient than another person who is trying to handle several tasks. As such, through the division of labour, delegation increases productivity. It would be a shame not to make the most of it!

What are the real advantages of delegation?

A project manager is not superhuman: they cannot do everything at once, as they risk not concentrating on the important tasks and making mistakes. The ability to delegate is therefore a real skill to acquire to optimise their time management and avoid being overloaded, or even overwhelmed. By entrusting tasks to their colleagues, managers can focus on tasks that are specific to their role. To do this, they must accept losing some time at the start in order to save time in the long run. This management strategy is often advised as part of burnout prevention.

Delegation is also and above all recommended as part of an overall team management strategy to improve the team's performance, make good use of the skills and experiences of all team members, and mobilise them to better motivate them. Indeed, entrusting colleagues with a task and making them aware of their responsibilities with regard to achieving an objective is very rewarding. They will feel that they are useful to the company and, as they become aware of their importance in the development of the company, they will be all the more invested in their task. Finally, by delegating some tasks to competent people, you ensure that they will be carried out well and allow team members to develop their skills. Ultimately, the goal of delegation is to succeed together.

STUMBLING BLOCKS

There may be a number of elements resisting this approach:

- lack of confidence in yourself or your colleagues;
- lack of time to define the objectives to delegate and the people to delegate them to;
- lack of skills within the team;
- lack of expertise in delegation;
- fear of losing power;
- fear of causing jealousy within the team.

These stumbling blocks create a vicious circle. There is only one way to break this circle: learning the rules of effective delegation.

PREPARING TO DELEGATE

It is vital that you do not wait until you are already snowed under before handing some of your work over to someone else, because this requires a good amount of preparation beforehand. As is the case before any decision, you should answer the questions "What? Who? How? Why?".

Define the tasks

Before diving in headfirst and delegating left, right and centre, start by selecting which tasks you can complete alone based on your workload and skills. Next, analyse the remaining tasks and sort them into those which:

- can easily be carried out by someone else (everyday tasks which have little impact on the rest of the project);
- require a particular skill;
- can be subcontracted to someone outside the company.

Take care not to only delegate the difficult tasks: you should also offload some of the more rewarding ones, or you risk demotivating your colleagues. Finally, you obviously cannot delegate the tasks which are part of the manager's role, such as conflict resolution, maintaining discipline etc.

Choose the right colleague

The next step involves choosing the person to delegate to. It is very important to choose the person who will be best suited to carrying out this task effectively. For example, it would not be productive to put an IT novice in charge of creating the company website, even if you think it would be a good experience for them.

Here you need to know the skills, potential, current workload, motivation and career objectives of your colleagues in order to organise your delegation in a way that benefits the entire team and encourages them to do their best. This approach is a team effort: it is not only about saving time, but also about putting yourself in your colleagues' place to help them to make progress and lead them to succeed together.

Start by going back over the list of tasks you want to delegate, then analyse your colleagues' profiles. Use a skills matrix to help you do this. It will give you an overview of the technical and human resources of your employees and will allow you to match each task to a particular profile.

Skills matrix

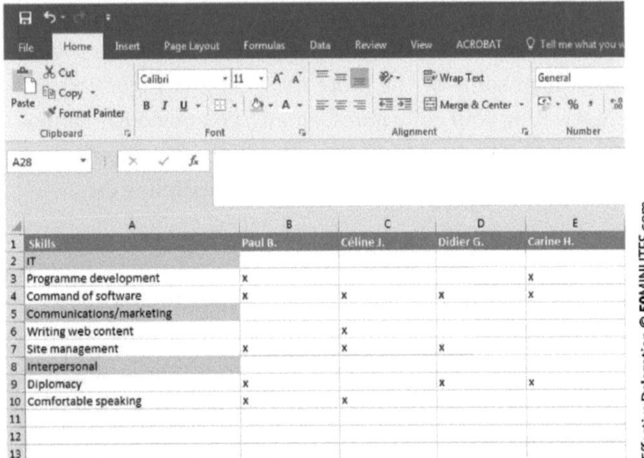

Skills	Paul B.	Céline J.	Didier G.	Carine H.
IT				
Programme development	x			x
Command of software	x	x	x	x
Communications/marketing				
Writing web content		x		
Site management	x	x	x	
Interpersonal				
Diplomacy	x		x	x
Comfortable speaking	x	x		

As such, for a project involving the implementation of a new advertising campaign, for example, ensure that the person you select has communication and marketing skills, as well as a list of advertising contacts that will be useful for the task. Once you have chosen the person, make sure they have enough time to devote to this assignment and that they are ready to get involved with the project.

Set objectives

Before you even think about informing the successful candidate of your decision, you must clearly define the task and the objectives to accomplish to facilitate the plan of action which is to be implemented. The SMARTE method will be useful for this.

- **S = Specific.** What exactly does the assignment involve?
- **M = Measurable.** How am I going to measure the results obtained? What will allow me to say that the result has been reached?
- **A = Ambition**. Why is it important to carry out this task and achieve this objective? Here you need to define the driving force behind your motivation.
- **R = Realistic.** Is the project doable? What means am I going to put at my colleague's disposal to ensure their success (money, training, materials, etc.)?
- **T = Time-bound.** What is the deadline for achieving this objective? Take into account the current workload of the employee involved.
- **E = Environment.** Although it is not always included (the best-known version of the method has no E), some professionals add this aspect. It involves checking that the project does not harm you or the company.

The SMARTE method

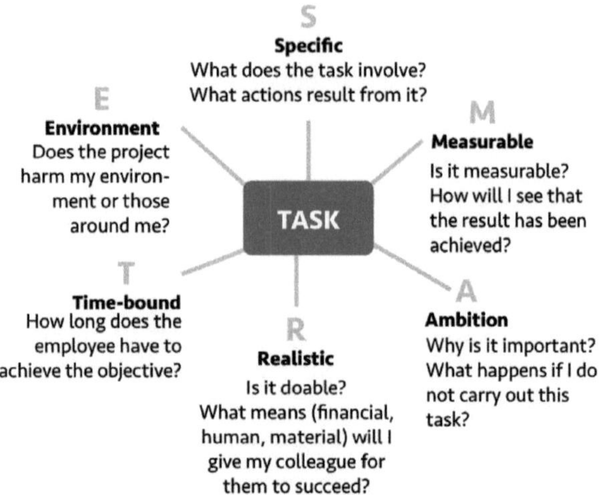

Example

We can better illustrate this process using an example. The director of a care home wants to organise a weekend in Alsace for 50 residents during the Christmas market period. He anticipates a budget of €500 per resident for transport and accommodation, but does not know how to finance the trip as a whole or where the residents should stay. Furthermore, he has no time to dedicate to this project. He therefore decides to delegate some tasks to his colleagues, with the main aim being to provide optimal accommodation for the residents while ensuring that they still receive the necessary care. He will entrust budgeting tasks to his financial manager, who is suited to this kind of work, and the transport and accommodation management tasks to his personal assistant. To organise his delegation, he first draws up a mental map:

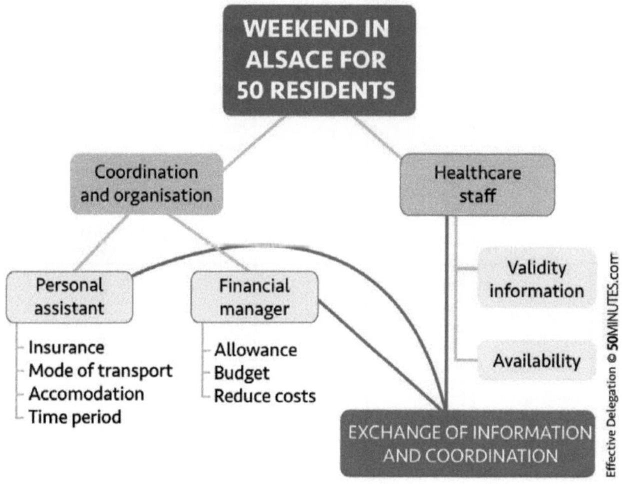

The director can also use a project evaluation grid, like the example below, which will give them a more complete overview.

	Overall project	Task 1	Task 2	Task 3	Task 4
Description and objective	Organisation of a weekend in Alsace for 50 residents of a care home during the Christmas market season.	Find a funding method at the lowest cost.	Identify a suitable mode of transport and accommodation for an optimal stay.	Find a mode of transport and accommodation which fit the budget during the Christmas market period.	Ensure insurance is organised and make sure accommodation and transport will be suitable for residents based on information provided by health care assistants.
Deadline	December of this year	Before booking; no later than end of August	August-September	September	September
Budget	€500 per resident; total budget €25 000	€25 000 maximum	€25 000 maximum (to be split between transport, accommodation and insurance)		

	Overall project	Task 1	Task 2	Task 3	Task 4
Skills	• Organisation • Finance and insurance • Management • Possible care	• Budget development and management • Knowledge of cofinancing	• Knowledge of residents' mobility and care needs • Ability to work as part of a team • Ability to supervise residents	• Analysis and observation of budget • Ability to research accommodation and transport • Ability to negotiate prices	• Knowledge of insurance
Potential colleague	• Personal assistant • Financial manager • Nursing manager • Occupational therapist	• Financial manager	• Nursing manager • Occupational therapist	• Personal assistant • Organisational ability	• Personal assistant

ENTRUSTING THE DELEGATED TASKS TO YOUR COLLEAGUE

Tell the person involved

Once you have identified the person who will carry out the task, you should arrange a talk with them to inform them and explain the details of the delegation. This is also the time to establish the framework and get them motivated. For the meeting to be as successful as possible and act as a springboard for what comes afterwards, it is essential to deal with a number of points.

- Explain to the colleague the characteristics of the project, such as the aims to accomplish, the financial resources allocated to the project, the material and human means at their disposal, the deadlines set and the obstacles they risk encountering. Clearly explain what you expect in terms of results and ensure that they understand fully. For example: "In our care home, I want you to see to the organisation of the new activity for our residents".
- You should also define with them the degree of independence they will have and the person to contact if the situation goes beyond their level of responsibility. As a general rule, the employee's room for manoeuvre will go hand in hand with their position in the hierarchy and their skills. Managers will tend to grant more freedom to a department head than to an administrative assistant. Conversely, if the team is made up of employees on the same level, the manager will adjust the degree of independence based on how much they trust the person. For example: "You can take all the decisions involving amounts of less than €2 000. Above that, you need to consult me". We generally distinguish six levels of independence, from the lowest level to complete freedom of movement.

Complete independence
The colleague only informs their superior during the evaluation meeting

Very high independence
The colleague acts alone and regularly informs their superior

High independence
The colleague carries out the actions then immediately informs their superior

Average independence
The colleague suggests ideas to reach the objective

Low independence
The colleague asks how to act

No independence
The colleague waits for the manager to tell them what to do

INDEPENDENCE AND RESPONSIBILITY

When individuals have little independence or little decision-making power, but are given major responsibilities, this can lead to tensions and damage the social atmosphere of the company. You must therefore take care to delegate tasks where the level of independence matches the level of responsibility. Do not ask a colleague to be responsible for a decision that you have imposed.

- Explain why you have chosen them and not someone else by mentioning some of their skills. For example: "You have several years' experience in this sector and you have organisational skills".
- Set out the importance of the project as a whole. This will allow them to understand why you are asking them to carry out a particular task and motivate them at the same time. To return to our example situation: "I am asking you to set up this new activity for older people, because we have a lot of requests from them and this development would allow us to stand out from other care homes". Another example: "Adding this niche would be very beneficial for our brand image and revenue".
- Finally, ask them what they think and negotiate any potential points that are a problem for them.

Follow up and assist

Following up and monitoring are an integral part of the delegation process. The goal is to make sure that the colleague has all the information they need, that they are motivated and that they have all the means necessary to achieve the objectives at their disposal. Your role is to help them succeed in the assignment that you have entrusted to them. Here are some tips for setting up a quality follow-up process:

- Set deadlines and plan evaluations during the process to straighten things out or adjust the approach taken if necessary.
- Lend your colleague an attentive ear and be caring towards them. There is no point criticising them for a small mistake; on the contrary, you should encourage them throughout the project.
- Put at their disposal training and tools that could help them in their task.

Debrief

Debriefing serves to evaluate the delegation. Congratulate your colleague if they met their objective and, if they failed, try to understand together the reasons for this failure and what they could have done differently. This is an important time for communication, so make sure that you listen. They may have had to face obstacles that they were not expecting. Or maybe the pressure was too much for them. Ask them about their feelings during the task and now that it is finished. Are they prepared to do it again? Is so, you will certainly be able to agree on further projects to delegate to them.

TOP TIPS

- Do not only give your colleagues the thankless tasks, but entrust them with rewarding assignments, as this will motivate them. The same goes for you: do not keep all the boring tasks for yourself, but establish a balance between the two. Furthermore, you should delegate the tasks that you do not have the necessary skills for and which would either considerably slow you down in the implementation of the project or would stop you from developing other actions. For example, do not try to create a computer programme yourself when you have an IT whiz who could do it for you in no time at all.
- Do not hand over too much responsibility at once to your employee, as this could stress them out and leave them flustered. Act gradually and in stages: give them a fairly simple task at first and then more responsibility as they become more confident. However, if the colleague already has experience and has proved themselves, feel free to delegate one or more tasks to them that they might subsequently delegate themselves. In any case, make sure that they agree to this when you meet with them.
- Entrust the tasks to a colleague that you trust, as much in terms of skills as professional behaviour. If you have doubts about a person, you will probably waste time by watching their work or fixing their mistakes, which would be entirely counterproductive and would harm both your relationship and the project.
- Leave your colleague free to choose the means and the processes to put in place to succeed. This independence

will demonstrate your trust in them, which will motivate them.

- Remain available. The person you are delegating to must be able to contact you and ask questions about any concerns about their tasks. If you are not available, you will slow the project down.
- Make sure that you follow the development of the project and give constructive feedback on the results attained or the areas for improvement, remaining consistent with your expectations. To do this, you could keep a logbook covering the role of each colleague, the division of tasks and how far along each task is. Setting up evaluation meetings is also recommended, as long as these do not take place too frequently.
- If something does not go to plan, review it privately with your colleague. There is no point reprimanding them in front of the entire team as this risks frustrating and de-motivating them, and causing them to lose all credibility with their colleagues.
- Avoid micromanaging. If you keep closely watching your colleague at inopportune moments, this will remove their responsibility and demotivate them. However, you must not delegate blindly and take major risks for the company. Quickly check on your employee from time to time.
- Avoid delegating when it is urgent or too late. Effective delegation requires preparation. Do not wait until you are snowed under before you decide, because your colleagues will feel as though they are being used as a last resort and will not get involved as you want them to. Take the time to analyse the project, define the different

actions to be carried out, identify the most suitable colleague, and communicate the information pertaining to the project.
- Do not forget to thank, congratulate and give credit to the employee. After all, if the project has succeeded, it is partly thanks to them.

FAQS

I DON'T FEEL LIKE I HAVE TOO MUCH WORK, DO I STILL NEED TO DELEGATE?

There is no point delegating for the sake of it. Do it when you have a heavy workload or short deadlines, or when a person is more capable than you of carrying out a specific task. Delegating part of a project is an effective way of successfully getting it done. It allows you to manage your time better and in this way to be able to dedicate yourself to other activities. Furthermore, by entrusting your colleagues with tasks, you make them aware of their responsibilities and allow them to become invested in the company's activity by motivating them.

WHEN IS THE RIGHT TIME TO DELEGATE?

Don't wait until you are snowed under or until you realise that you will not be able to achieve the goal set (through a lack of time or skills). As soon as you get a new project, analyse all the skills and tasks that will be needed to see it through. Identify the ones that you can handle alone and entrust your colleagues with the others. In addition, take advantage of slow periods to organise your delegation of power.

WHEN I DELEGATE, AM I ABANDONING PART OF THE PROJECT?

Contrary to what many people think, offloading some of the tasks does not mean abandoning the project. It is a necessary method for better organising working time by dividing tasks and responsibilities. This allows you to reduce stress while showing your team that you value them and motivating them. Delegating is the complete opposite of abandoning; it is a way of giving yourself the tools to see your project through. Forget the clichés and try it!

CAN I ENTRUST MY COLLEAGUES WITH ANY KIND OF TASKS?

You can delegate in any domain: administration, sales, finance, marketing, technical, etc. What counts is knowing what you want to hand over to other people and selecting the best colleague for the task based on their skills, their availability and the amount of responsibility involved. You should, however, remain responsible for tasks which fall under your role as the manager. Finally, avoid abusing this approach by delegating tasks purely because you find them boring.

ONCE A TASK HAS BEEN DELEGATED, DO I STILL NEED TO DEAL WITH IT?

Monitoring is necessary whenever you delegate, provided that it is done in moderation. Indeed, it would be counter-productive to closely watch your colleagues' progress on the project every day and to inspect their slightest actions and movements. It is better to plan evaluation meetings, although these should not take place too frequently so as not to slow down the process. These meetings should be accompanied by positive feedback to allow your colleague to continue on the right track. Rather than monitoring, it is a matter of guiding them in the success of the project.

WHAT TOOLS CAN HELP ME TO ORGANISE MY DELEGATING?

There are no specific tools for delegation. However, using mind maps or tables to divide up the tasks can help you. Remaining positive and available, communicating at all times, making the necessary resources available, and encouraging and believing in your colleagues will be your best assets to succeed.

WHAT RISKS ARE LINKED TO DELEGATING?

Although delegation is often recommended as a way of lightening your workload, speeding up the process of putting the project in place and showing the staff of a company that they are valued, it brings with it a number of risks, such as:

- disrupting the hierarchy, in that the decisions made by subordinates could take priority over those made by superiors or may lead to contradictory messages being communicated;
- creating jealousy or resentment within the team;

- causing deviations from the norm if the person delegated to abuses their power or if the person doing the delegating hands over just any task;
- causing frustration for the person who the task has been delegated to if they are not guided well or if the objectives are not clearly defined.

HOW CAN I MAKE SURE MY COWORKER WILL ACCEPT THIS TASK POSITIVELY?

For the person to accept the task you are giving them positively, you must ensure that they do not see it as an unpleasant assignment that you want to get rid of. Explain to them why you have chosen them (what skills), present the importance of the task to them and grant them some degree of independence to carry it out. If you involve them in the project, trust them, make them aware of their responsibilities and grant them some initiative, they will feel valued and will fully commit to the project.

CAN DELEGATION BE REVOKED PARTWAY THROUGH A PROJECT?

An act of delegation established for an unspecified period can be revoked at any time. If a person is abusing their power, you can absolutely take it away from them. It is also worth remembering that delegation is linked to actions and decision-making. This means that the departure (whether natural or not) of a supervisor who has delegated some of their tasks or responsibilities does not automatically bring about the end of the delegation.

DO I NEED TO FORMALISE MY DELEGATION IN WRITING?

In the case of a transfer of power, it is strongly advised that you formalise this delegation in writing, specifying the date that the transfer of power takes effect, the duration, the nature of the powers delegated and the potential agreements defined in advance by the delegate (the person entrusted with some of the responsibilities) and the delegator (the supervisor who is transferring some of their powers).

In other cases, such as the delegation of tasks on an occasional basis, it is not necessary to draw up an official document. However, it is important to remember that any written records may be useful in the case of legal action and could be used as evidence.

OVER TO YOU

You now have everything you need to delegate successfully and benefit your entire team. To help you get started, use the project grid or a mind map to decide what tasks to delegate and who to entrust them to.

Project grid

	Overall project	Task 1	Task 2	Task 3
Description and objective				
Deadline				
Budget				
Skills required				
Potential colleague				

Mind map of a project

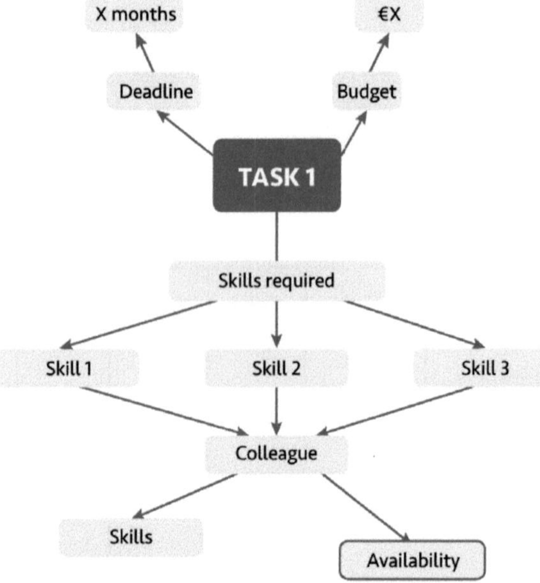

We want to hear from you!
Leave a comment on your online library
and share your favourite books on social media!

FURTHER READING

BIBLIOGRAPHY

- Condis, S. (2011) Comment déléguer en 5 questions clés. *L'Express*. [Online]. [Accessed 21 November 2016]. Available from: <http://lentreprise.lexpress.fr/rh-management/management/comment-deleguer-en-5-questions-cles_1525738.html>
- Coudière, H. (2015) Savoir déléguer pour réussir. *La Formation Pour Tous*. [Online]. [Accessed 21 November 2016]. Available from: <http://www.laformationpour-tous.com/comportemental/pratiques-outils/savoir-dele-guer-pour-reussir.html>
- Segeco (2010) *La délégation de pouvoirs dans les sociétés*. [Online]. [Accessed 21 November 2016]. Available from: <http://www.segeco.fr/base-documentaire/la-delega-tion-de-pouvoirs-dans-les-societes-sp_fiche100112_1.html>
- Tramond, P. (2009) Sachez déléguer. *Pilotis*. [Online]. [Accessed 15 November 2015]. Available from: <http://www.pilotis.fr/extranet/upload/presse/78%20OCT%2009%20NOUV%20ENTREPRENEUR.pdf>

ADDITIONAL SOURCES

- Genett, D. M. (2004) *If You Want it Done Right, You Don't Have to Do it Yourself: The Power of Effective Delegation*. California: Quill Driver Books.
- Heller, R (1998) *How To Delegate (Essential Managers)*. London: Dorling Kindersley.

- Keenan, K. (2015) *Delegate: Learn How to Let Go with Confidence and Get More Done.* Bath: Pocket Manager.
- Smart, J. K. (2002) *Real Delegation: How to Get People to Do Things for You – And Do Them Well.* New Jersey: Prentice Hall.